Skulls + Bugs Adult Coloring Book

Relax and practice mindfulness with the beauty of the human skull.

Fourteen beautiful designs await your favorite pen, crayon, colored pencil or marker.

Printed in the United States of America
First Printing, 2016

LifeSlice Media Publishing
PO Box 91293
Columbus, Ohio 43209

AdultColoringBooksandJournals.com

I0473040

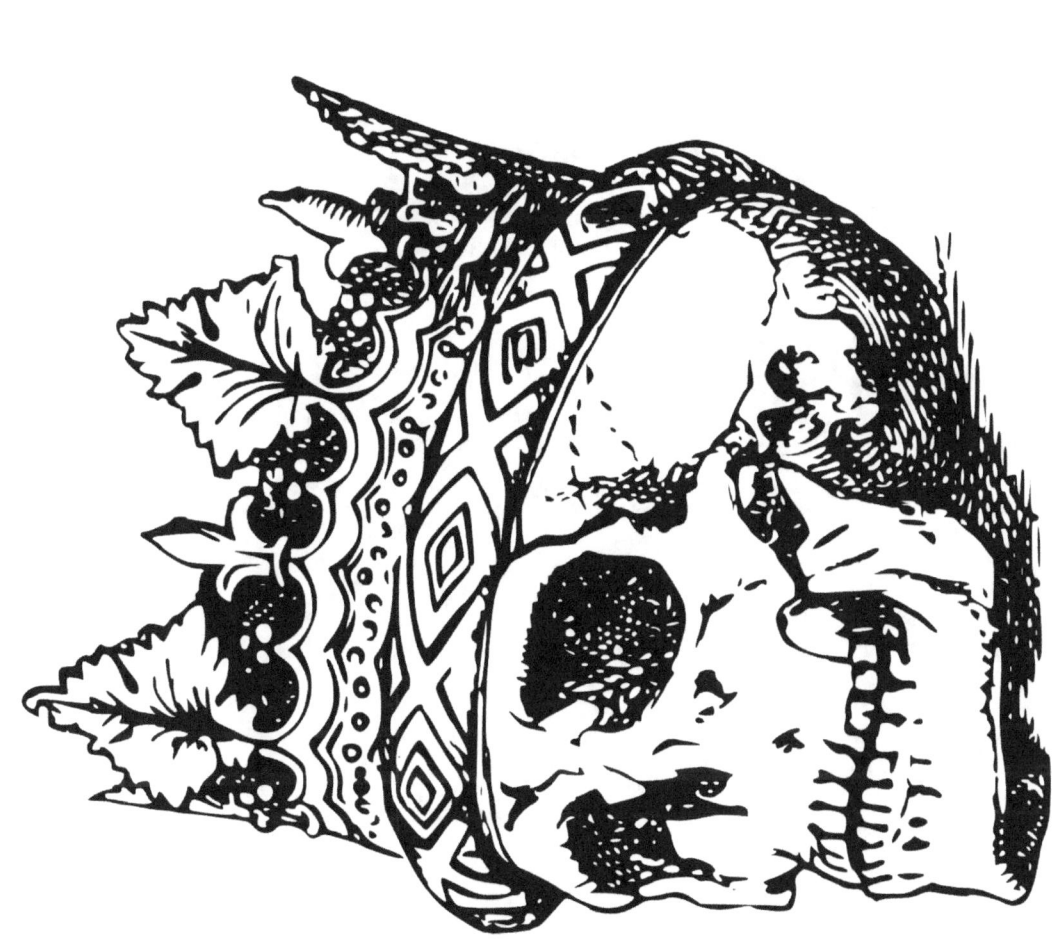

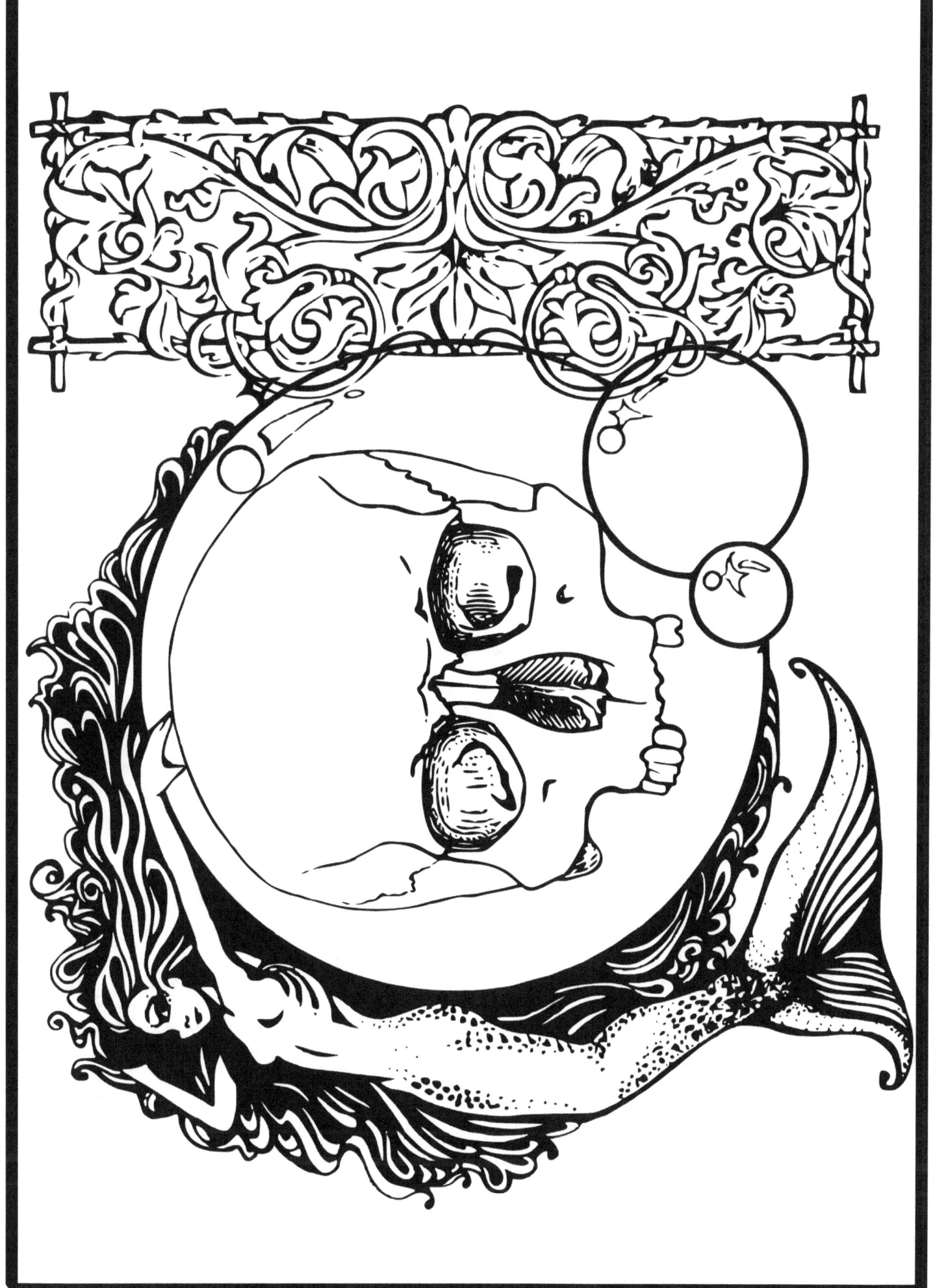

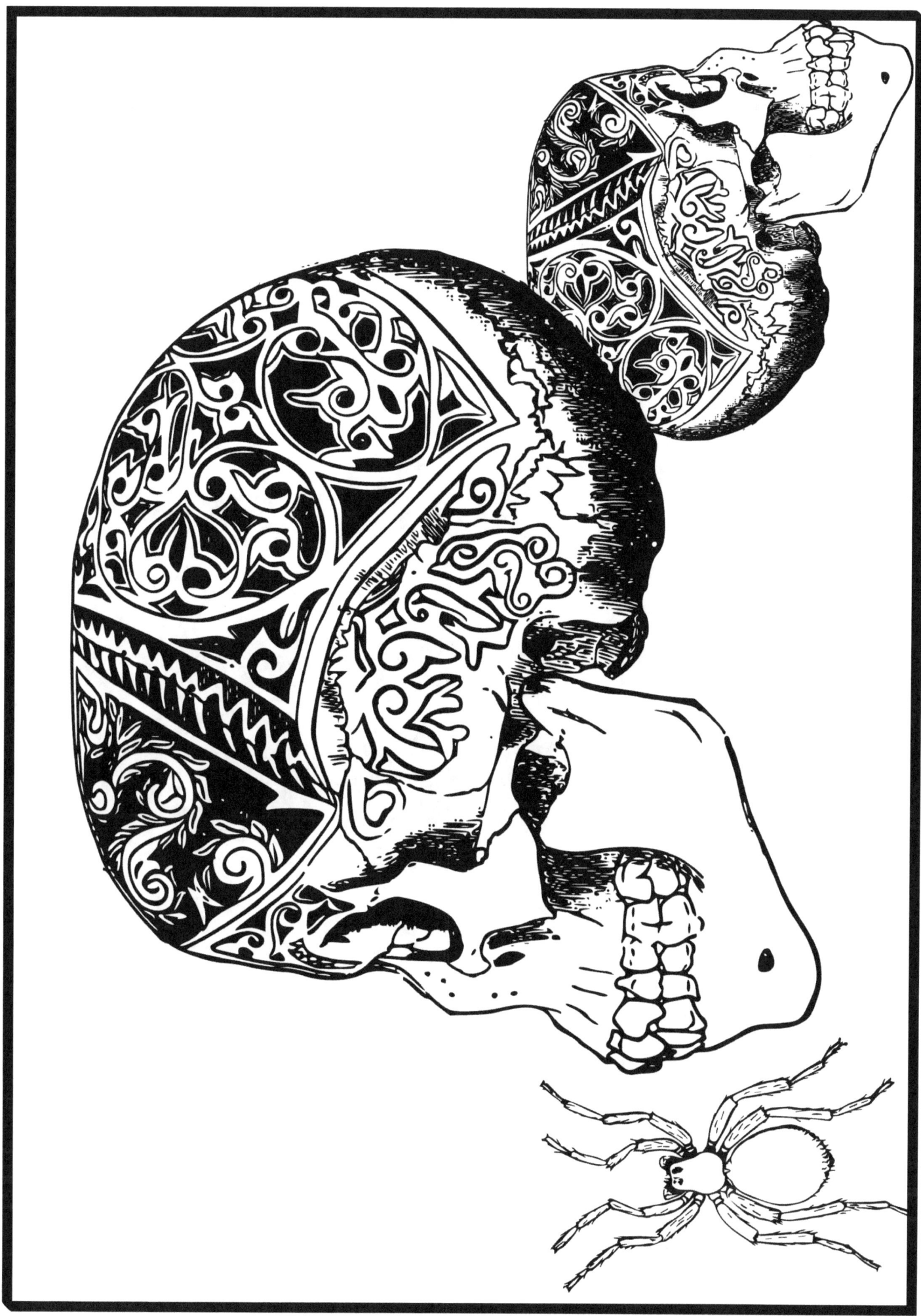

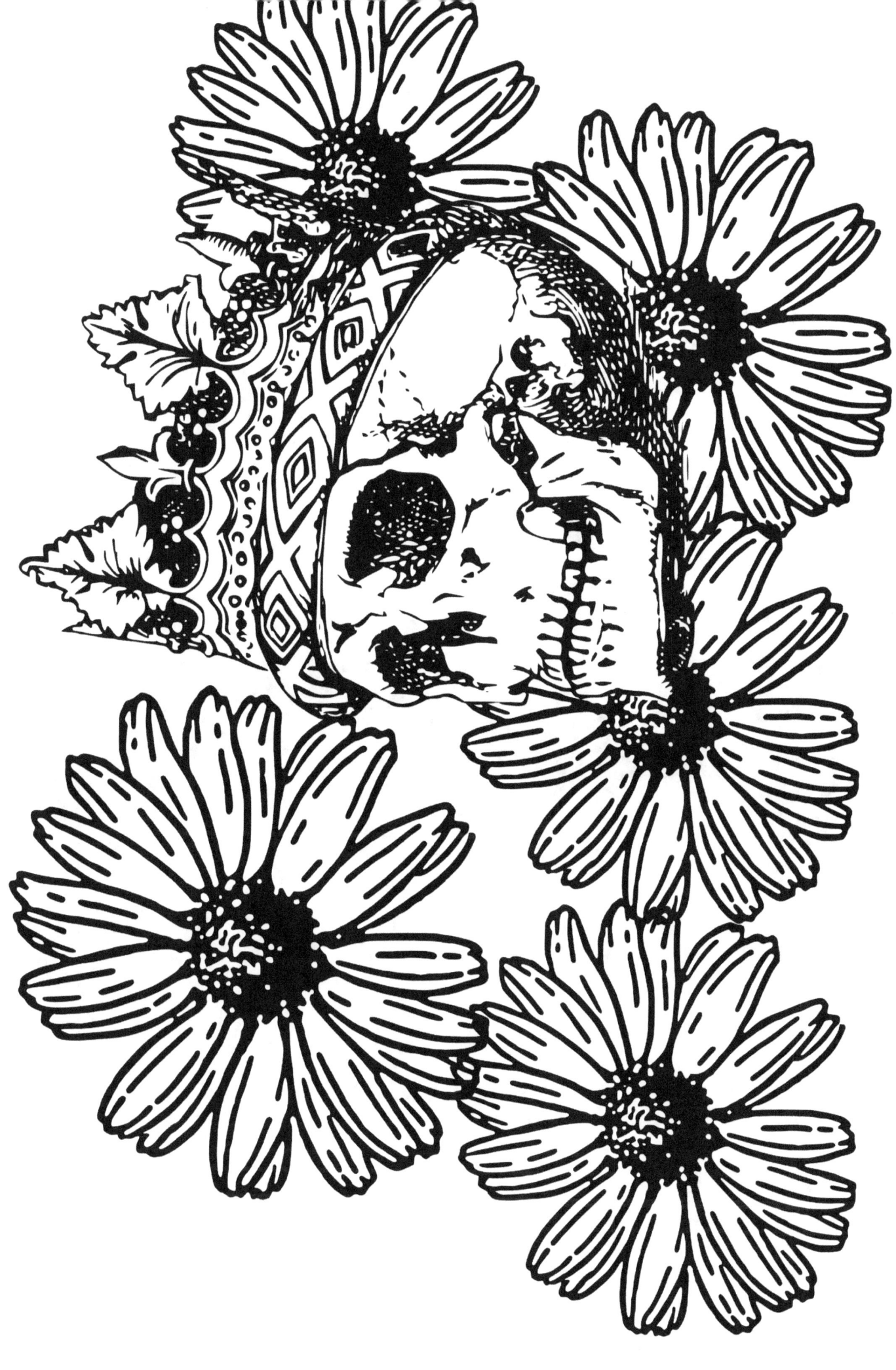

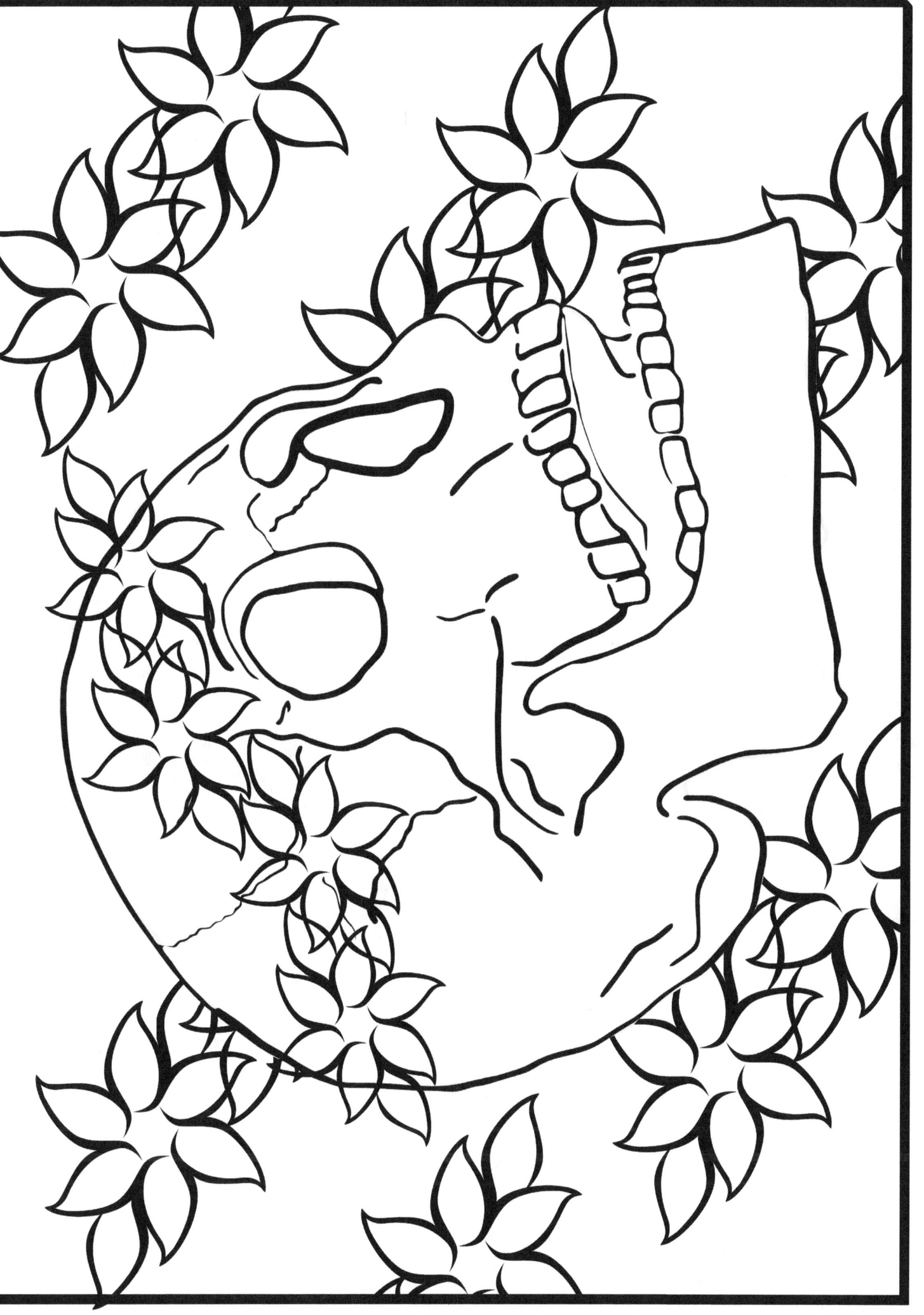

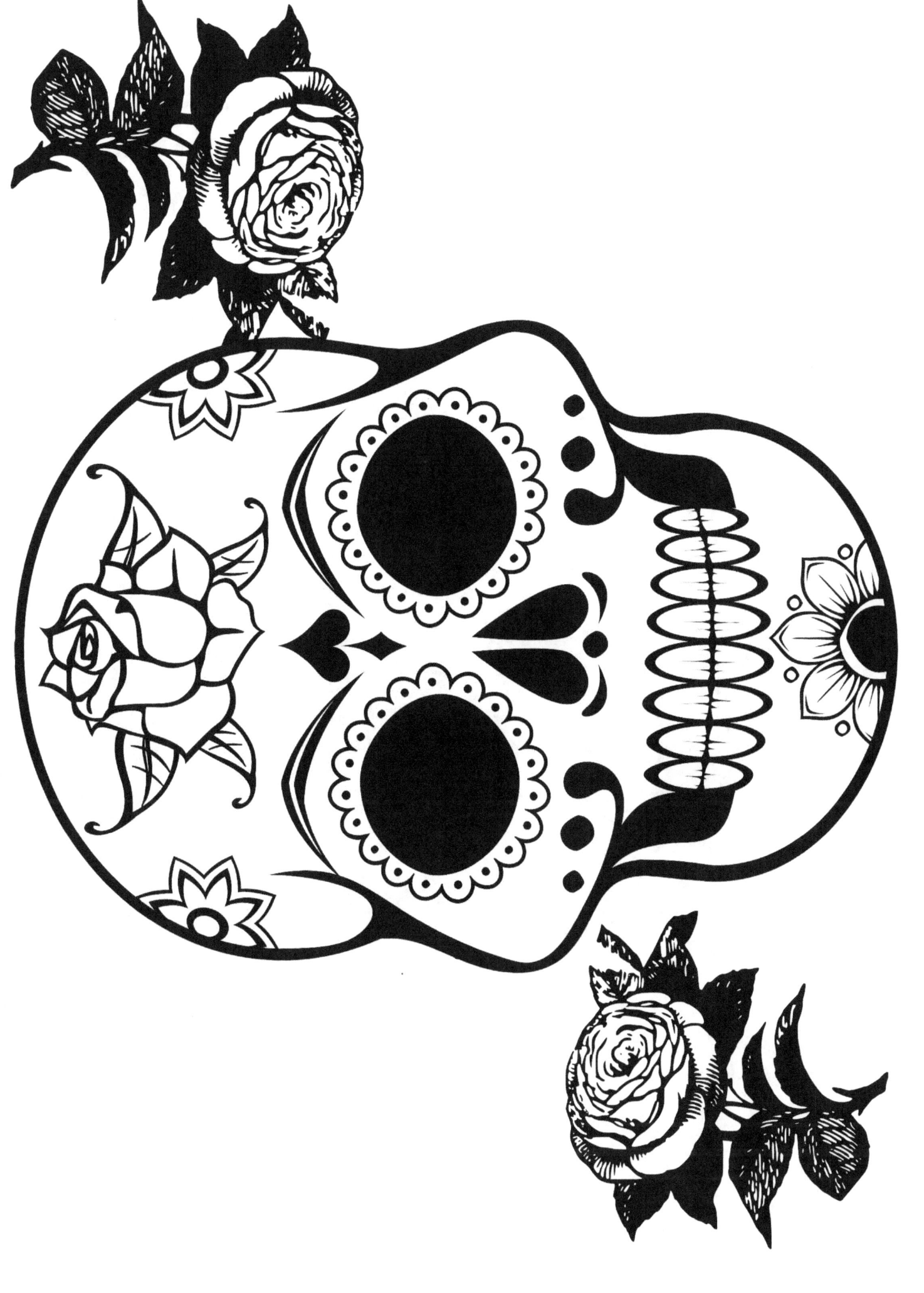

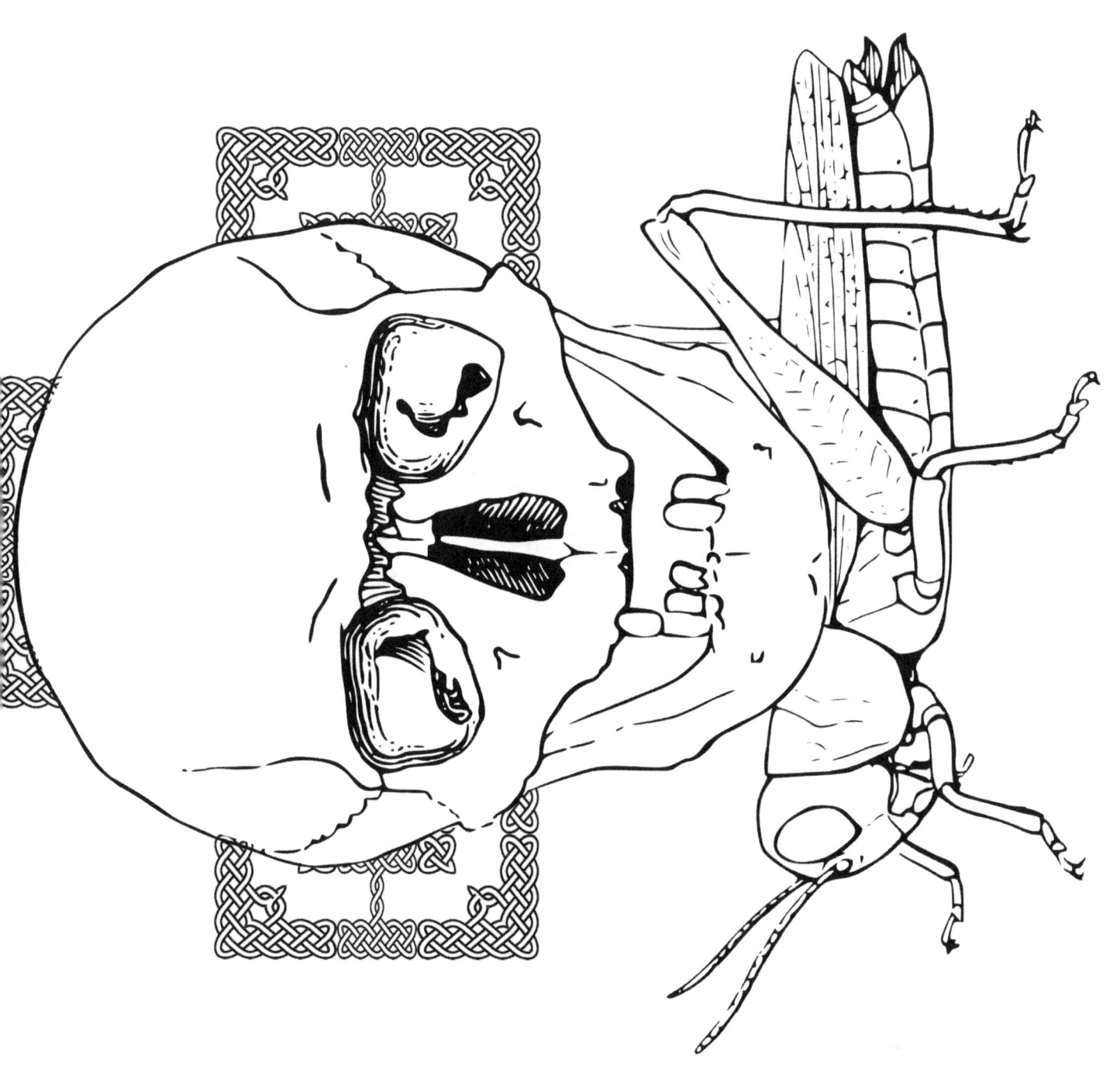

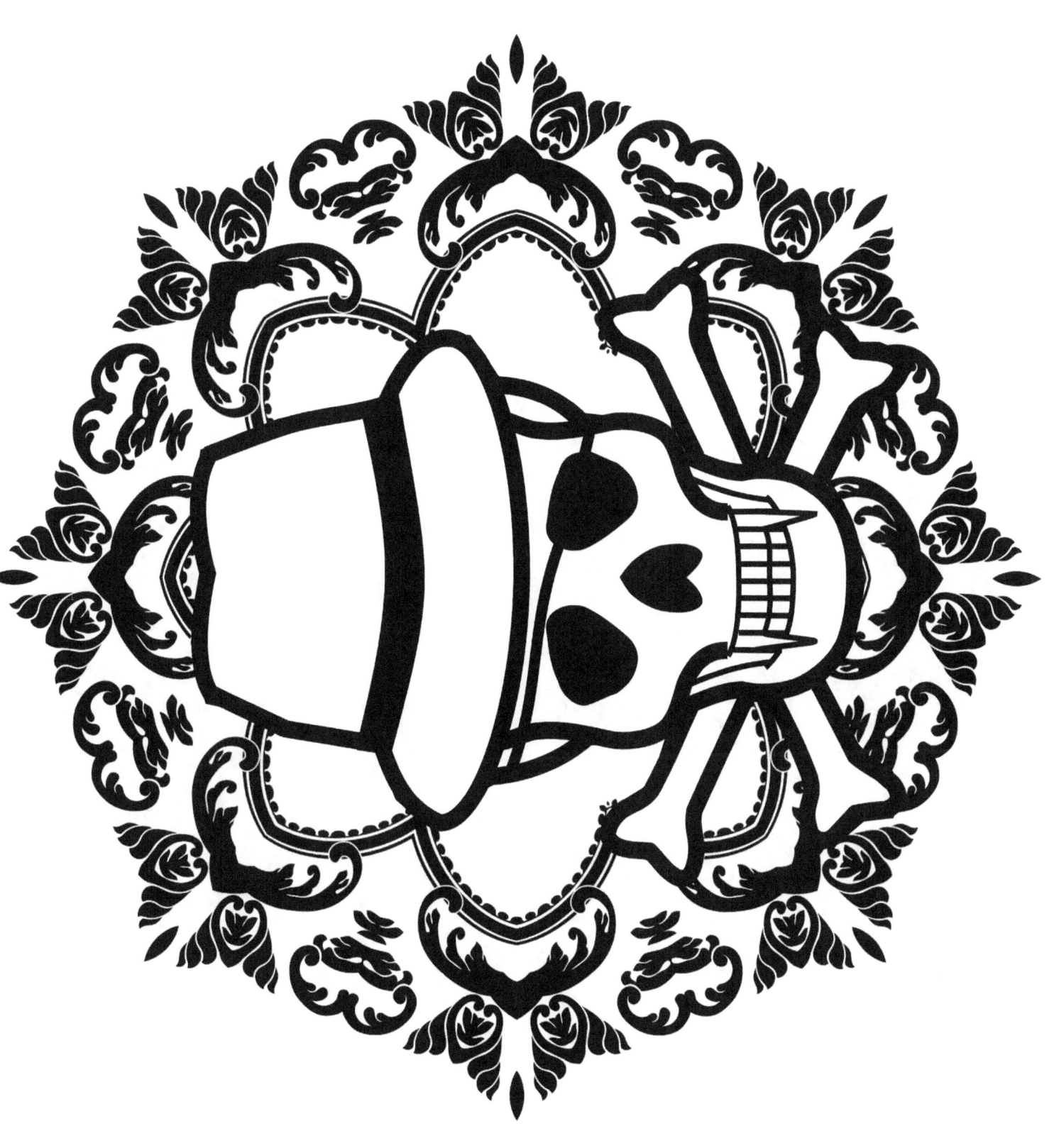

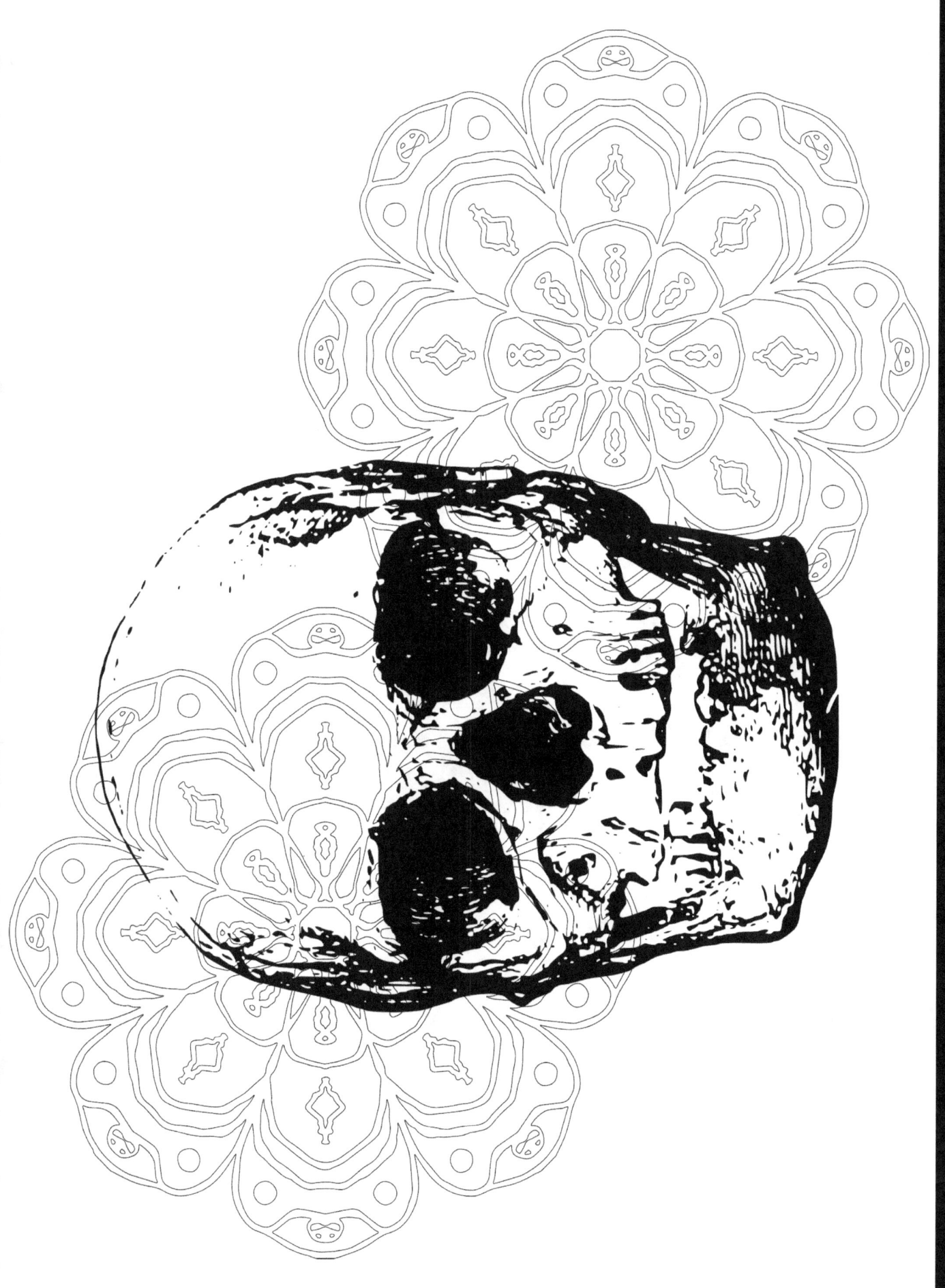

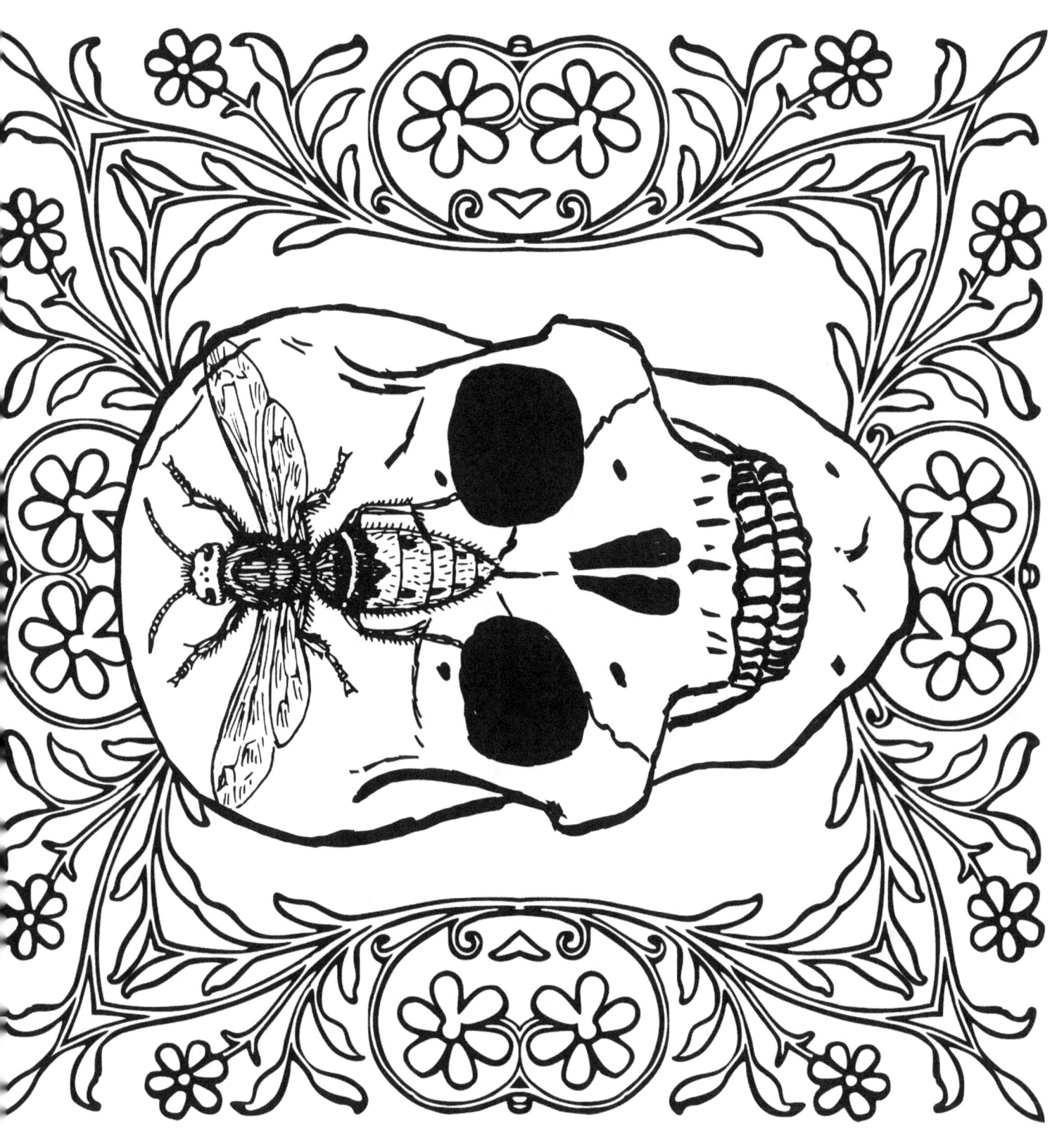

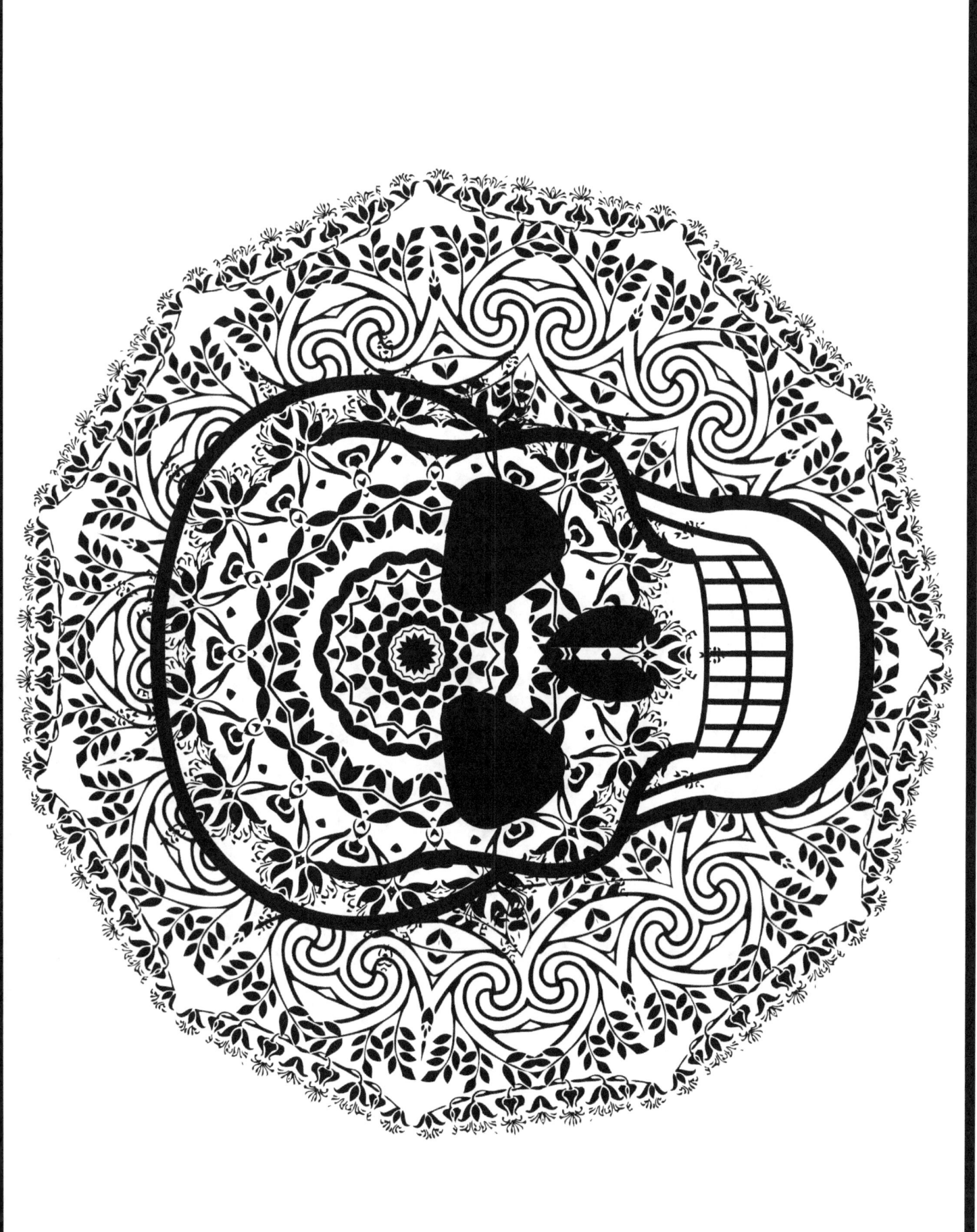

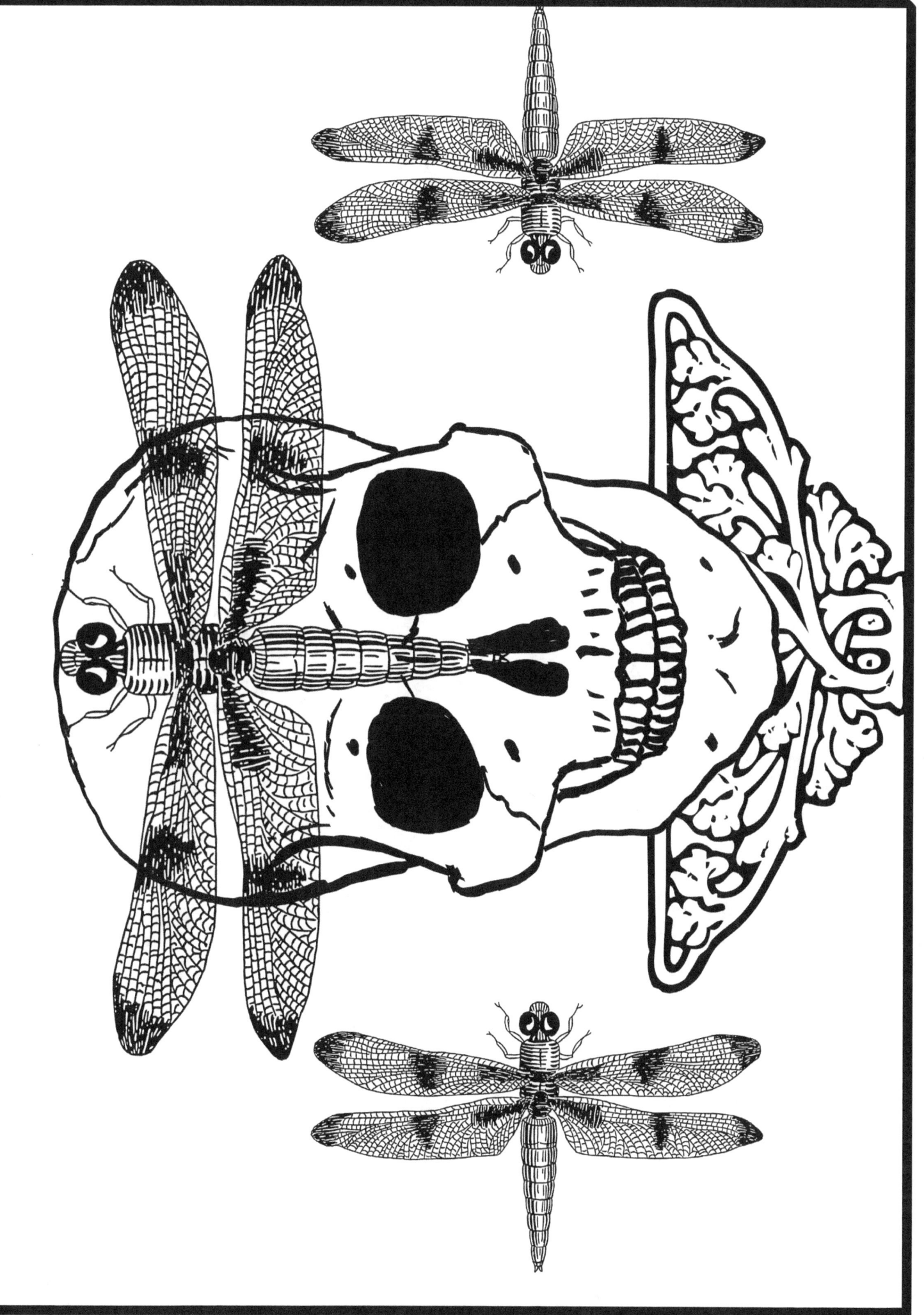

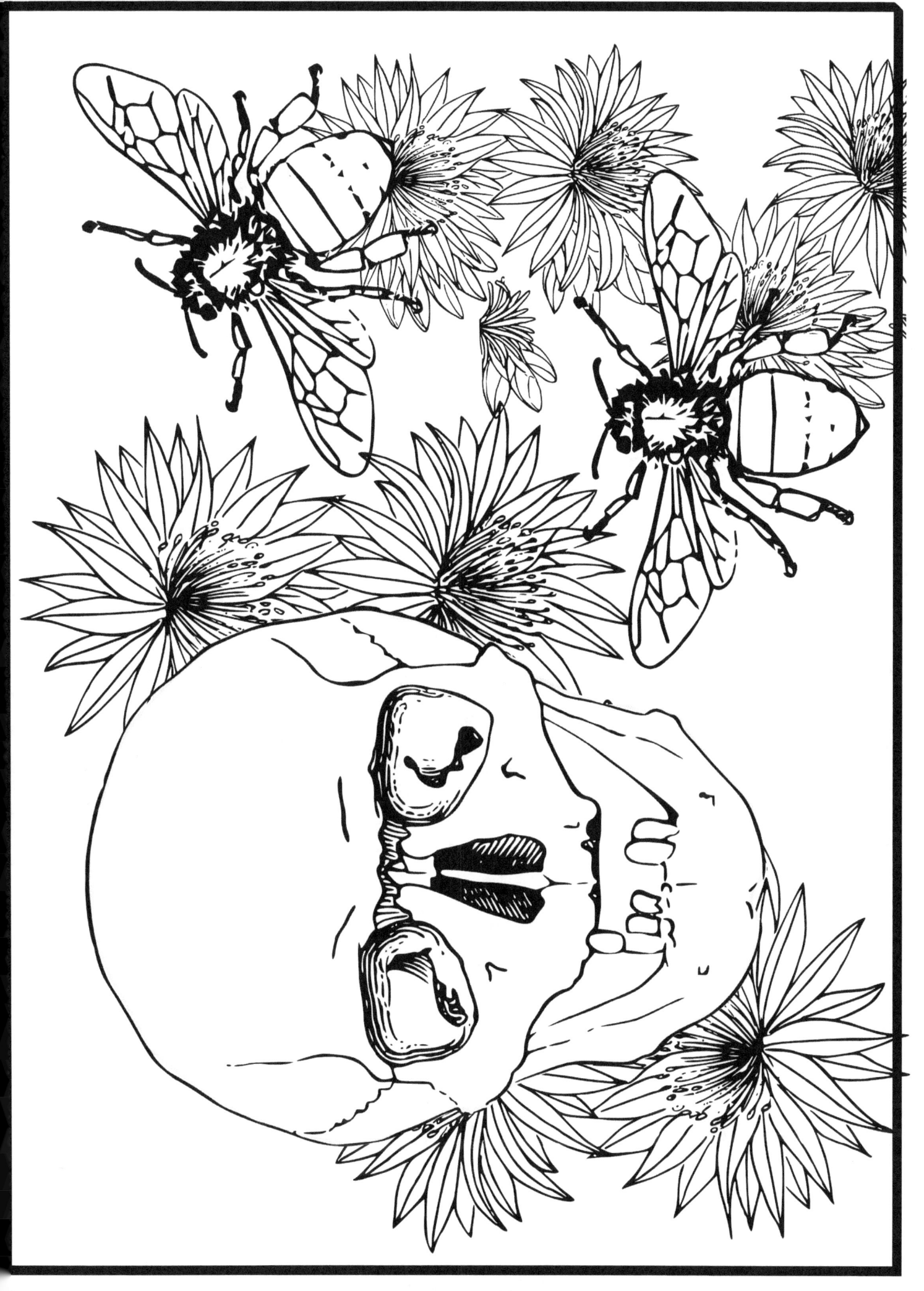

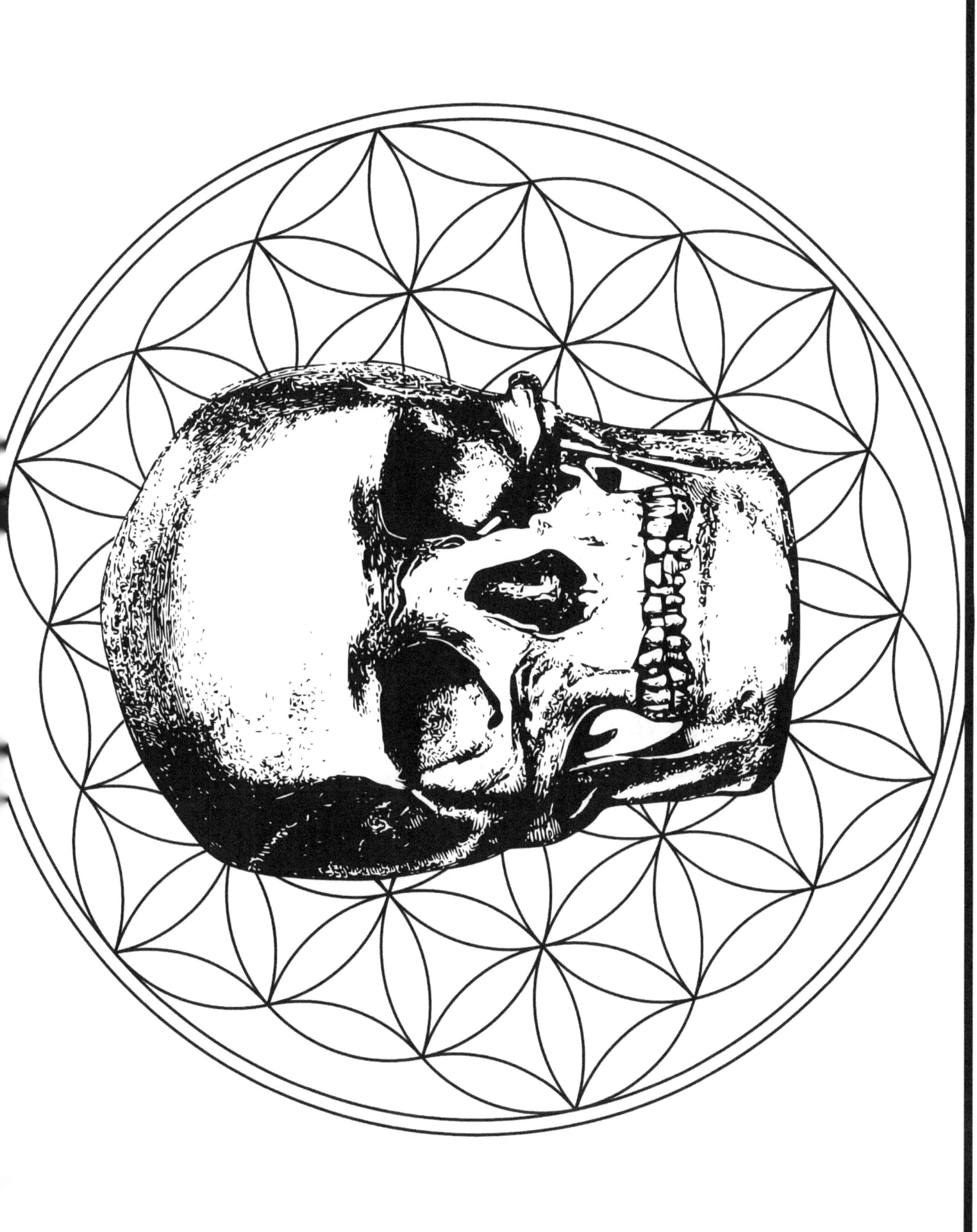

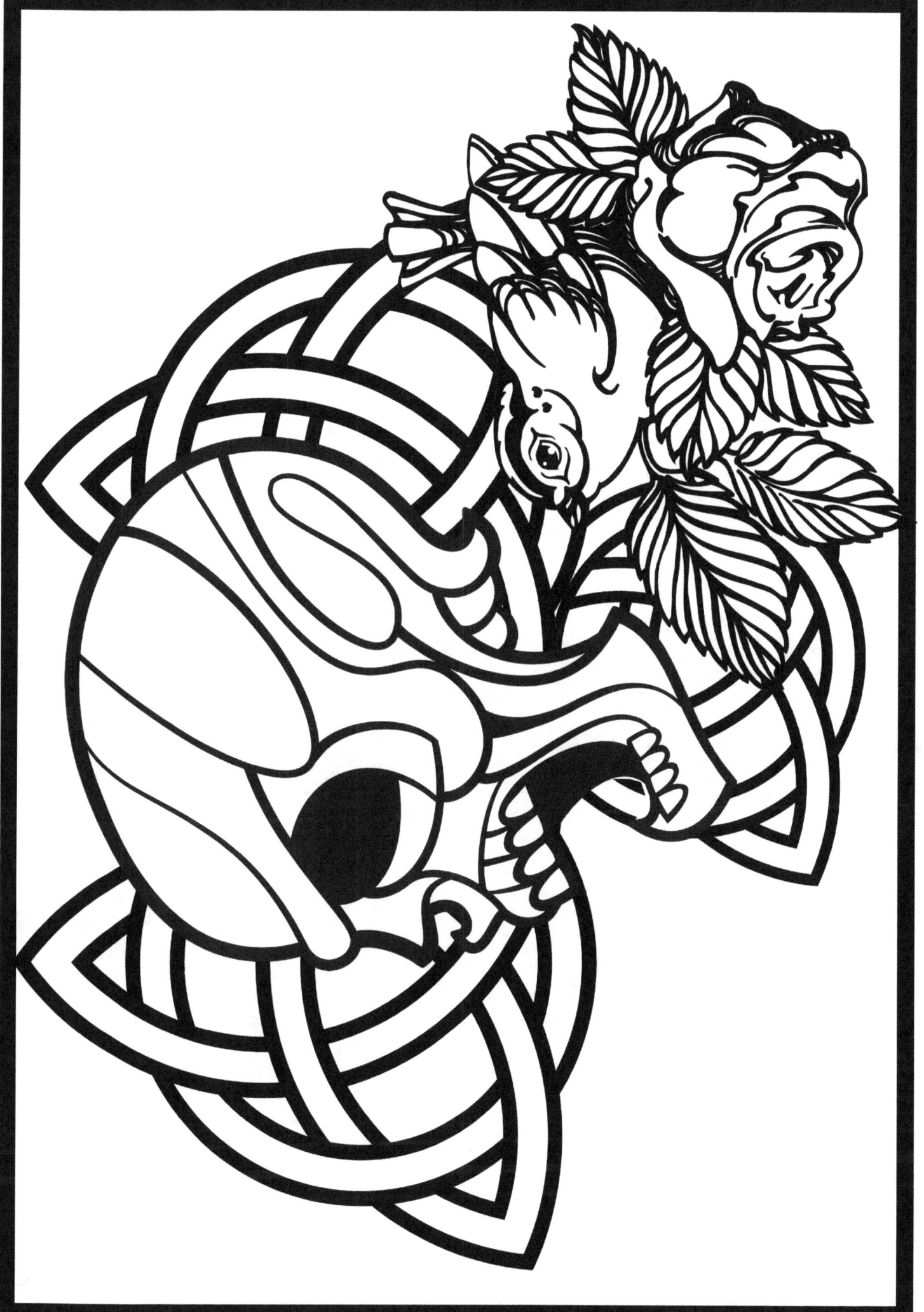